Hidden Lakes

and

Dragonflies

Roger Dale Reynolds

HIDDEN LAKES AND DRAGONFLIES, Reynolds, Roger Dale

1st Ed.

Edited by Farley Dunn

Cover photography by B. J. McCoy

 THREE SKILLET

www.ThreeSkilletPublishing.com

All characters are fictitious, and any resemblance to actual persons living or dead is purely coincidental.

This book may not be reproduced in whole or in part, by electronic process or any other means, without permission.

ISBN: 978-1-943189-25-0

Copyright © 2016 by Malania E. Reynolds

All Rights Reserved

"On a thread not long ago, I was reminded that, whether we believe in fate or not, whatever we write is fated, by its nature of being a story. This made me think of the odd and seemingly incompatible differences between fiction (what we wish for, perhaps) and reality. I think we do what we can to bring the good parts of our fiction and fantasies into real life, but even that has unforeseen consequences."

Roger Dale Reynolds
July 16, 1969 – October 20, 2010

— *Part One* —

Sitting in the Corner

— *Part Two* —

Darkness Is Me

— *Part Three* —

Pop Corn Box

— *Part Four* —

An Evening Ride

— *Part One* —

Sitting in the Corner

— A WORD UNSPOKEN —

For snow-covered mountaintops
I would run.
For teardrops rolling down a crooked smile
I would spill my blood on the sand.
For that one word I want to hear
I would give my last breath.

It's a good thing we haven't met,
Because I can no longer
Chase the mountain passes,
I won't give salt for salt
Or lead for lead
And I don't know how to say—

— UNTITLED —

Bumping June bugs,
A carpet of crickets,
And an unaccountable cacophony
Of cicadas
Summer.
But what I love the most makes no sound.

On low walls, on the steps of the back porch, and on
The lichen-covered rocks.

The gecko sits
Until
At once
As if his eyes see all sides,
He runs!

— FIRST TIME —

Finger to her lips, we leave
The coffee table society and,
Hand in hand, pass between the dreamers and drunkards
Down the hallway and through the door
Into each other.

— EXPLORATION —

A room with one window
The sunrise floats above the moon shadows
Clinging to those under the influence
Of words and unspoken other things.
Those shadows aren't for hiding, not this time.
They're for exploring. It's a safari into the wilds of each other.
It's a voyage over the edge of a child's fantasy world.
Here there be dragons. And winged horses.
And treasure.
The sun sneaks around the curtains for a closer look.
But, this is when the hiding starts.

— BOUQUET —

It is walks too fast for me.
It hears a voice too soft.
It is she was, and will not be.

Be for me.

A hollow choices made;
A hollow resting on her side; I hear the sigh.
A hollow leaving again; this the last?

Come and go; do not stop.

Wilting roses grass between her toes.
Wilting roses blinks an evergreen eye.
Wilting roses she was and will not be.

Be for me.

Forest run, laughing! Forest fall, kissing flowers.
Forest fire, marshmallows on sticks, and warm sleeping bag.
A leaf strides past her cheek, she smiles!
The hollow is that smile-stop thinking!

No use, today crawls back inside.

It is sits with her friends.
It is drinks shots with funny names.
It is she, and will not be.

Be for me.

A hollow numbers, exchanged.
A hollow waiting, that's all.
A hollow throwing pennies at windows.

Came and went, but did not stop.

Wilting roses lace covering her hair.
Wilting roses tears fall on the diamond.
Wilting roses we were, and will not be.

Be for me.

— THREE LITTLE WORDS, THREE LITTLE WORLDS —

Screams of laughter—bliss of innocence.
Whimpering spoilsport-eternal inexperience.
New day every day, not always fun and play.
Supercalifragilisticexpialidocious.

Whispers of covert actions—rebels by night.
Reading the tale of hope-shoot 'em on sight.
Youth and wisdom, authority and boredom.
Antidisestablishmentarianism.

Speeches of ridiculing rhetoric—finally officials.
The older the bolder—the longer the initials.
Smallest movement, reaction of deadly intent.
Abracadabra.

— FROM THE CHAIR —

Anal retentive resurrections
Never meant much to me
Forgo the forget-me-nots;
I won't need them
Where I am going.
There's only—
Dandelions puffed and flying
Then no greater can be conceived.
Dodecahedrons; a deadly secret,
Towers growing in all directions.
Failure means not wasting enough time
Drinking honeysuckle
While the pretty girl
Holds out her hand.
Great minds think awake
And dream in Technicolor,
While Sunday morning worshippers
Talk to themselves.

— STAB —

Frank words hurt and humble and
Bore
       through
              the meat
                     and
                            into
                                  the bone.

— THE SEER AND THE DREAMER AND THE MIXING OF DREAMS —

Smirking like I know something you don't.
Whoa, wait! You missed it.
Far-seeing takes time. But then the vision hits like a lightning bolt.
Gorgon reflections within. Watch myself turn to stone.
Bang! The dreaming and the turning and the turning
Away.
Icicles stretch from back-length hair . . . I'm nowhere.
Slice! Through and through, the sword of Damocles breaks its thread.
How fortunate.

Within the dream, water runs round and round your breast,
Exactly as airplanes and starships encircle your head.
Messages in bottles broken against mighty titans,
And lovers in titans broken against icicle mountains.
Should they find the lifeboats, they may follow me
Into the savage forests of the new world dreamscape.
Into the noble fictions of eastern papermongers.
Out of the blue event horizon and into the black lagoon,
Where unbroken titans nevertheless find their final resting places
On shelves above the fireplace in the house of yesterday.
Today and tomorrow intertwine like hands on a melting clock,
Then slide down the wall beside the fire
Easily, creeping
Over the smoldering coals;
Only to be rekindled as another yesterday.

But you sit, warm in the big chair.
Your face barely visible within the folds of a granny quilt.
Your mind tracing the history of every patch.
Your eyes glittering in the firelight.
What yesterdays do you see in the flames?
And what tomorrows?
Smirking like you know something I don't.

— TRIPLE POINT ON THE THIRD ROCK —

Not in vain, no
Nor hiding in windblown cups
Dancing in the rain!

Same, same and same again
Drifting through the days
Then nights found on Berry St.
Dancing in the rain!

From silence and star light
The comets fell into sound.
From snowflakes and rippling streams.

— FRAMES OF REFERENCE —

Yes, that's what I said,
Forever.
Now, don't go being that way;
If it don't last, it don't last.
Just don't forget that once you got me to say,
Forever.

— WAKE UP AND SMELL THE MILLENNIUM —

Do you just write to see the cheetah gnawing on a bone?
There's but one reason to drag a wheel up the side of a crater on Mars.
Someone out there is watching!

Or . . . Or . . . Or maybe the habit's just too hard to break?
The life on the lam, the lamb on the pita, the Peter Principle.
The name in print.
Without this, who would be the one to spray water and methane
On the ring between Mimas and Rhea?
A whole universe to come home to.
Sure, your car's losing oil, but have you seen the drops on Hellfire
    Peninsula?
Man, the blues and greens are filling my slots like bad science on Cable.
Don't give in to the transpose of the matrix of co-factors.
Don't fall into a rut unless you're the Alpha female.
Even then, a lioness might ring you on her cell.
So fine, so firm, so fully functional right out of the box.
A baby's not a miracle, but who can watch the Learning Channel
Without getting a splash of blood in his eye?
And there's the outside insanity of it all.
Eels in a Japanese butt.
Box cutters on a plane.
Oh, wait, that one's for the red tide slowly seeping into the Ambrose
    Channel.
If you don't get any of this,
I'm right with you, Bud.
It's all a mystery to foregone conclusions.
It's all a dream to the All Devourer.
It's all for one, and one for the road.
So, let's go!

— HOMEWORK —

e
for effort
i heard that
somewhere once.
all i ever got was
i
incomplete thoughts
spelling errors
Capitalization in Inappropriate places
run-on sentences
fragments grammatical clusterfuk
okay they never used that word
but even that would have been better
than
f or d
or even a C+
at least it would have said
you tried.
but what the hell can i do with i?
that only means there's more work to do.
sigh.

— THE OTHER SHORE —

There's an island
At the end of the world
A lonely stone
From where can be seen
The birth of a cloud
And can be heard
The howl of
The suicidal sea.

Sit there beside me
And I will share with you
My golden spyglass
So that you might also
Glimpse
The other shore.

— THE OTHER SHORE II —

Frosty mugs clinking;
Good times before the voyage.
I take a stroll down by the slips;
Murmur of water against razor sharp inboards.
No fog but foghorn blowing
Distant . . . my soul.
Lights sparkle between horizon waves;
The stars are voyagers, too.

Won't you?

Morning bright;
Leather hands pull at hemp.
Spinnaker flies.
Roll, pitch, and yaw;
Swaying into the sun.
Tacking against the wind.
Hanging on the trapeze;
Dipping my back into the waves.

Won't you?

Nearing the edge,
I run aground
On the last shoal.
Climbing the stone
Of farsight,
Fingers dislodge memories.
No more time for home fires;
The sun sets eternal cascades afire.

Won't you?

The stars my destination.
The jewel of new mornings within my grasp
And nights of milky madness
Call across the abyss.
I alight upon mists of silvery moonshine
And cross to the other shore.

Won't you?

— THE OTHER SHORE III —

The serpents bow and curtsy before my love,
Their wings rippling in the summer breeze
Upon the shore.

The sun glistens within teardrops
Shed by my happiest, hopeful love
And burst in Lilliputian fireworks
On the sand.

Her bare feet follow mine
From beach to grass to cool stone;
The doorway, the winding stair.
Her hands hold the filigree railing, but her hair flies free;
Her eyes search for the world we left behind.

Then back down for another formal greeting.
A withered man in a mage's cloak;
Exchanges of knowing glances.
I came across when dreams were still new, he says.
She smiles;
She knows my dreams are younger every day.

She, upon a roan;
I, upon a dun.
Given both with only tales for payment,
Knowing we'd never return for the telling.

Evergreen butterfly wings
And finer things
Await our questing souls
On the found continent.
We turn our backs to the abyss
And follow the ancient path
Up between the dunes,
Into the trees,
Into songs sung by our mothers,
Saying: welcome
To the other shore.

— HONESTY —

Words work
A wicked way
And seldom mean just what they say.
Even when spoken in bonds of truth,
Hidden intentions can lead them astray.

— MY PLAYGROUND —

Ruled by the past, I return to the park.
I remember this place; not faded quite yet.
Even the darkest night spent in this small forest
Shine forever in my memories.
The creek, silently and slowly flowing here; gurgling
Softly over rock dams there; and sometimes seemingly
Dry. Never over three feet deep; even the lightest
Of beds; I used to think it wasn't-couldn't be-planned.
The creek comes from storm drains and ultimately
From people's lawns, streets, and gardens. I didn't think
Of that somehow, when I was young; when I would come
To this park; when it was a plaything of my mind.

— LINES WRITTEN ON THE WEB —

Fallacies and fricassees and faculties
Lounging in the back room;
Far away from the kids
Far away from responsibility.
Don't even try to understanding comes slowly.
With exotic, esoteric eschatologies knocking down your door.
You don't even need my penny-ante ramblings
Sew, Y R U reading it?
There, but for the Grace, Space Ace,
I'm bored too.

After all, there's no one I'd rather see again than
Your once upon a time
There's no greater love than that between
Paisley and Chantilly lace.
There's no higher calling than to fight for
The Lasting Impression.

There's the the and the who and the
WTF are you talking about?
I'm talking about the birds and the bees and the flowers and the
You.

Funny thing, that word with only three letters,
Second person, singular.
Neutral in the mother tongue
But implied feminine in this poem anyway.
I'm not making a connection, though, Amirite?
So, I'll just take a
Right where the calendar's wrong.
Seven
Eight
Nine
Ten.

— WATER —

A stream flows slowly.
The water does not move
Molded to the gravel.
Pulled free of its
Grave bounds,
It quickly reforms
And falls back home.
A silent, man-made waterfall.

— DOVE —

Where in lies—
The prize if the ayes
Have it?
Wherefore art thou
Romeo if you don't know
Family from foes?
Whence comes love
If not of pity on this little ditty
Or even a snow white turtle dove?

— PRETENSE —

Wordplay
On a sunny day
When I should be far a__
Thought you knew what I should say?
How about another try
At figuring out why
The perfect girl with the perfect guy
Still says a little white l___
Come on, you didn't think it
Would be that easy, did you?
Over hill,
Over dale,
Let's hit the dusty t___ .

— SEVENTEEN —

As if you didn't bring it up first!
Silence in her face, at least.
Freight cars streaming past for miles,
Their wheels sound just like tornadoes.
Smokey lungs and empty pack.
Fidgeting with the lighter in my pocket.
Will this never end? Try again . . .
So, you said you broke up with him?
Her eyes roll. Chugchugchugchug.
No getting to this one.
But, isn't she cute?
And this is the perfect time.
Indiana Jones would know what to say,
To a girl standing beside her bicycle,
Waiting for the train to go by.

— UNTITLED —

The one you love—
The one you know
Can't rise above
The ebb and flow
Of testosterone,
And can't be shown

Your simple love
To him unknown.

So lower the veil—
Your billowy sail
That hides in him
Both Heaven and Hell
And look through new
And shining eyes
To where the true
Surprise lies.

— OUT THERE —

bottleneck narcolepsy
rastafari fur
betelgeuse and bullet holes
gen X excalibur
funky, funky
cum junky

— MY THOUGHTS ARE —

My thought are
scattered as wishing was
when windows in schoolrooms were
open.
—outside the windows now
wondering what the children see.

Once storm drains were lunch time escape
down to danger park
where the creek ripples
and birds sang.

Will wishes still fly through the halls
and scatter across soccer fields
seeking solace in the park
when books are traded for keyboards
and windows for flatscreens?

— SUPERNOVA —

On the belt of Orion, space is not cold;
Here there be dragons,
Thrown from the buffeted nursery,
They consume themselves in blue-white heat
Biding their short time,
Bloated in rage and revulsion.
They wait only until they taste their overload.
Then gather themselves together into inconceivable fury
And spray death upon a million worlds.

— PERCH —

Red iron staircase
furry flora shower stalls
in the sandstone canyon
won't bring back hiking
no matter how clean the air.

Wheels big and casters small
armrests and contoured seating
a throne fit for
the hanged man.

— GOD-SHAPED HOLES —
(AND THE THINGS THAT REALLY FILL THEM)

Freedom in a bottle
Tastes too much like
Truth written in smoke
Smells too much like
Prophesies written in blood
Only foretell more death.

Look in the rocks instead
Smell the flowers red
Listen to the bees
Buzzing.

Screaming for silence
Sounds too much like
Killing for peace
Looks too much like
Praying for wisdom
Only reaches the ears of ignorance.

Look to the skies instead
Walk on other worlds
Watch other suns
Rising.

— NO PINNING ME DOWN —

way out in county downs
for the fey not frowning clowns
headed for four
twenty's a plenty
their sound abounds

walking forests from within grinning
growing forth
fondly gone winning
someone better become fun
or dancing girls will desist sinning.

don't in this serious frame be tame
lest spurious worries set your name aflame
in same way be gay
beat friendly fire at the same game.

welly well, I'm outy to be lame again
with fame in my name and restrained and sane
it's not to cry about anyhow
no pinning me down in the rinsing rain.

— WE WERE —

We were

—nibbling rose petals
and the pretty girl said it
only hurt when she
picked one.

—happy in the cold rain
because, even on the bad days
the mention of a rose's name
made her laugh.

—bathed in all the scents of folded flowers
from first bud to the last fragile memory,
pressed in a book.

—mirrored sparkles in a drop of dew
clinging to a wild beauty
clinging to a garden wall.

—she said
weren't we?

— OFFER OF COFFEE —

what if I said
horsehairs and cool clover
hairy spider legs and muddy feet
a day called summer
a night with the cat's secret name
she breathes it in your ear
but you can't hear
such a soft sigh
with such a fast-beating heart
so it starts.

what if I said
hay barns and bay mares
empire builders and ant farms
a town called yesterday

a city with more faces than doors
she touches your hand
but she's with the band
such soft hair
such a shame she isn't there
when the lights go down.

what if I said
piano keys and twisted trees
crumbling cliffs and a stiff breeze
a room called waiting
a bed with more ghosts than pillows
she looks into your eyes
but only until the taxi arrives
such a soft voice
such a kind way to say goodbye.

what if I said
no thanks instead.

— WAITING —

Irises bloomed where now long grass chokes the view,
But the bulbs remain. Delicate the word
Once used to give voice to their beauty.
Delicate the touch that gave them their softness.
How long can the bulbs be held down by yellowed swords
Before the lips open and speak again?
How many weeds must scratch the skin
Before white velvet is caressed again?

— UNTITLED —

Sickly is the sweet smell of religious freedom.
The bones of the blind mingle with the ashes of truth.
They prayed for The End, so be it.
Who can mourn for those who know the answers
To the questions we all ask?
Through whatever path
They've gone to God.

— FANTA'S EYES —

See Fanta's eyes
And plagiarize
The fleeting song they play.

Soft colors weave
Sigh and deceive
Yourself; she knows the way,

Within flowers
And autumn showers
She gathers golden intent;

Through deepened wells
The virgin's bells
Ring visions heaven sent.
The New Romancer,
Wouldn't answer;
She shows a hint of mirth.

Is it the eyes so rich
Or shall a witch
Pull you down to earth?

Gaze in vain
Through infinite pain;
You don't know that surprise,

The history
And the mystery
Which hide in Fanta's eyes.

— SCHOOL DAZE —

A door closing,
A brush of cold air
The sounds of high heels bringing in the day.
Click-clack, click-clack.
Down the hall someone waits. For what?

A group of kids. Talking, walking, bored.
A couple in a staircase. A little bit early for that, don't you think?
A locker closing.
First bell.
School.

A door opening.
Warm sunlight.
The sounds of traffic urging me home.
Honk! Honnnnk!
He still waits, alone.
Same kids waiting for buses. Talking, standing, bored.
Same couple in a car. Will they never stop?
Throwing books in a locker.
Last bell.
Thank goodness!

— UNTITLED —

Walls of wandering,
Ceiling of sky;
So is the wind and so its reply.

The two became one
When a third falls away
Where go the snowflakes, no one can say.

Trapped by vagrancy,
Bounded by dreams,
That answered so quickly is not what it seems.

For love to be lasting,
It cannot be shared,
Or giving or taking, the pain will be bared.

The air is frozen,
But my skin is not chilled.

— FAITH —

A simple trust in one divine
Has this girl of flowing hair;
Belief in love incarnadine
And clemency beyond compare.

Still fresh with freedom, she's trying her wings;
Asking no help, but giving her best.
Alongside her dear brother, she happily sings
And all who hear her love her, so well is she blessed,
We could all learn from how well she is blessed.
The beauty of He who was slain on the cross
Shows through in her eyes and her generous smile;
For no matter material distress or loss,
She thanks the Lord Jesus for life all the while.
With love and allegiance she prays all the while.

Through devotion informal her worship defends
The idea that Jesus will triumph again.
In this profane existence she stands by her friends.
And humbly holds her fond vision within.
Though tempted and taunted, she holds it within.

She strives to transform her soul into one
That conforms to an ideal essence of pure,
But I know that already it shine like the sun
And so shall forever endure.
By divine grace may it forever endure.

Thank you for giving me this reason to love you,
And thank you again for being my friend.
For I know that if God should finally prove true,
You'll surely go to meet him in the end.
And Jesus will meet you there in the end.

Why was I born without this great faith?
And why can't I find such contentment as she?
Am I in death to become a torn wreath
To follow sad courses for all eternity?

— SNOW —

Crystalline H_2O
Fallen opera
Closer look reveals
The dance of light
Still goes on
Until, like the white rose,
It fades and dies
In the hand of a child
Who grew
The parent of a snowflake
That gave it life.

— MY MUSE IS —

Nineteen for a week.
None for the reaper.
Three for the girl winging her way into other people's memories.
Or were they really for the ones whose words those wings have built
Because she lives?
Too many for my selfish self
Two more for my pride.
How many for nothing at all
But for the sheer joy of uttering joy?
Oh, but, death has had his day, you say?
But my finger move not a scythe.
Oh, but somewhere meaning was lost in between one line and the next, you
       say,
But my mind saves logic for equations far less colorful.
If only there was more than this
And that and all we've heard before, you say.

Not you who think you are!
A break in the day is all I ask;
Scant few minutes and you can go back to your friends and your gossipy
       communities and
Not-safe-for-work careers.
A rip in the routine;
All my fidgety nonsensual saucery
Isn't it enough that you don't know what I'll say
Metaphorically speaking?

— GLASS —

Shattered
Broken
But not completely
Disturbed.
It is still silent.
It still does not move
By itself.
Wait. Don't walk.
Ouch! It bit me!
Revenge.

— TWO BETWEEN THE TREES —

With fingers intertwined
We walked through the park.
Did you hear all the birds?
We needed no well-crafted dialog.
Did you see my smile?
We needed no lanterns, torches, flashlights.
Did you feel the night wind?
We needed no winter overcoats.
Without even a purpose beyond warming our palms,
We walked hand in hand.
Do you remember?

— ALL OVER THE PLACE —

Dipped hands into the Crater Lake
I'm drinking the cold blue . . .

Delicious sight, my only love!
My pen at play.
Oh, yes, this watering hole for the synonym-starved,
This craven of ice, translucent.
This lava tube in the side of Pele's throne.
Unleash your bitters, your sweets.

Where else can I find such fruit,
Spice, and pepper in the same dish?
Yet, finish hungrier?

Unlace your undies and let the flesh breath;
Create in my mind's eye those things usually only glimpsed at peak.
Failing the intricacies of seahorse valleys,
At least show me a snowflake or two.
Fly me on leathery wings
And illuminate my way to your bright eyes.
Don't let my thoughts dwell on a single
Isle in the midst of the lake.
There be the home of wizards.
I want to make my own magic.

— TURNING PAGES BETWEEN MY EARS —

Far from yesterday
Waste not wanting this to end. Granted handshake wishes
I'm yours for the
Pull me into your heart
Treat me with surgeon's bathysphere
Cover my myopic my hallowed sound
Canticles can't with fresh—they're forgotten sidelines
Guilt in gold, the domes enclose
Not ghosts, no. Win ever you play
You will lease the dogs of
Forged steely eyes wandering two paths
Unknown
Overgrown with scissorhand hairstyles
Watching out gubernatorial wills legislating in the aisles
Bake s'mores over hot tin roofs
Blown tornado uppercut
Really kicks me in the
Shins & grits
Just a way of turning pages between my ears.

— SITTING IN THE CORNER —

Sitting in the corner,
Sitting with my back against the wall,
Sitting wherever I want because that is my fate.
Sitting where I can see you
Trying not to see me fishing the shadows
For others like me who can sympathize
With their tired eyes
Looking for just the right place to sit.

Love may come from sympathy,
But never from pity,
Never from cat-scratch insults
Hidden in polite platitudes;
Never from those little conversations
Centered on a table across the room.
Never from the flitting of moths around a candle
Though there's always a candle and the inevitable moths.

Never from the writing of poetry
Though the reading may bring admiration,
(Or more likely admonition from the moths.)
Never from the taste of sweat
Though millions have thought so.
Never from sitting in the corner
So why do I do it?
I'm watching the couples and the candles
And asking how they hold the attention
Of the infant oracles
Asking why they gaze so longingly
Into the flames.
Asking who can sympathize
With half a man
With half a heart
And half of an excuse
To be sitting in the corner.
I can sit wherever I want.
It's my fate.

— *Part Two* —

Darkness Is Me

— THE EDGE —

I've ridden long, dark roads to find a place to hide
From alienation I have caused; an evil voice inside.

I'm safe from pain of brothers lost; and sisters cried.
I think I've come to bow to none; no one abide.
But the subtle guilt begins to creep,
And invades the world within my sleep.
The wicked grin is born again; I remember how well I've lied.

The force that draws me in my dream cares not for mercy mild;
I'm shown the landscape of my thoughts; the streams and woods defiled.
The sun above me has no face; the clouds pour tar.
The plants are frozen, twisted death; I've gone too far.
Then I'm reminded the show's not over, but I see my soul run wild.

— BOX —

The first day the first cigarette came before breakfast.
The first night the first light of dawn found you surprised.
The first week after your first kiss stabbed your inner child to death.
The first year you can't remember your last birthday.

Once upon a time, you had all your pictures in a box.
Then you bought a diary, a scrapbook, a cork board,
And left your box in the dark corner behind your coats.
But now you can't find enough words to fit your pictures into your dreams.
Your scrapbook is full of other people's faces,
And when you look for pins to use on your cork board, you find
The box empty.

— NIGHTS AT THE DOG STAR —

Swaying to the sound
Of something only vaguely resembling music,
Calling out
Your criticism of the singer's girlfriend's hair
Lips an inch from my ear
Your eyes wide;
Brighter than the stage lights.
You never knew when you were the most beautiful.

— FOOL'S GOLD —

Will following your long, lost lover
Bring you any closer to home?
Will wrestling with angels
Or dealing with devils
Or leaping on a Leprechaun
Put a shine to your soul?
I only ask because—
I don't believe
In angels
Or devils
Or little green men.

But I'm still looking for love.
I'm still trying to get home.
And, I'm still rubbing on
This tarnished little nugget
Of fool's gold.

— FACE IN THE WINDOW —

I was off on some meaningless tangent,
Giving my attention to code and ugly dudes in the Blades Edge Mountains,
When I just happened to clicky . . .
And you were gone.
Years past, you were no longer down the street and around the corner.
Distance more than time, separated by the arched gateway,
Yet your face is still there in shadow even now.
Your eyes . . . to say it would be smoke rings in the morning fog.
Your lips . . . of course there are the other things, but these words are
      foxholes;
I can hear the bullets flying, though I can't see them.

Don't go. I thought you were gone before, gone to the midnight sun,
But you only went far enough to lose—

Again, the tracers fly; a warning shot to silence me.
I thought you were gone again, then a voice spoke the secret word,
And here you were, your voice barely above a whisper, but still your face
      before me.

Don't go. As long as I know you're out there,
I know there's a world I want to be in.

— SUICIDAL SYMPHONIES —

Leaning towers on barstools,
Withered flowers and homesick fools,
At the Hop.
Golden showers breed naked cesspools
At the Hop.

Words to the wise whitewash the walls
Indirectly.
Witness as the witless huddle in the halls,
Mystery to me.
Follow the faithful finding their futures,
Wishing to be
Eternally free.

Remember the Axis at Main and Magnolia
Over the hill.
Hear the black dances cordially control ya!
Against their will.
Pawing and paying—they're puking, not praying;
Knowing they will
Eventually kill.

Financial forces are focusing;
Hare-brained homeless are freezing;
Miracle on Berry.
Warning! The children are breeding;
Miracle on Berry.

— FANTASU (DEAD GENIUSES) —

Words of promise; locked in hardcover;
Story begin.
Reading the fiction of stolen reality;
Inquire within.
A Bible for the New Age, the Gospel of the Sun Sage;
Wicked one, turn the page—wages of sin.

We didn't write the words;
Passive in fact.
If the authors are real;
Only then can we act.
Living someone else's time; borrowed from the byline;
Rescued in the nick of rhyme—evil ones jackal.

Just when the gettin's good;
Dead without trial.
Happily ever-aftering;
Silent denial.
Deadly inner world extensions, easing more realistic tensions;
Living on in sick conventions—Living in style.

— UNTITLED —

The white dove flew,
The warm winds blew;
And then she came.
My soul heard screams
That tore its seams;
She had no name.
She killed the dove
And then my love
She did tame.
She turned cold
This girl so bold;
She gained her fame.

Then she was gone
And I her pawn
The final shame.
Nothing she felt;
The cards were dealt;
I'd lost the game.
My soul cried.
My heart died.
No one to blame
But blind old fate,
Who could not wait,
And, so she came.

— (TO ETHEREAL SUICIDE ARTIST) —

Why give death such high praise
When dying might not end your days?
If the religious are truly right,
Then death does not end your fight.
The one you can only lose
Because by winning death, you cannot choose
How lives will bend.
You only choose
Your life's end.

— UNTITLED —

I decline
Through puffy clouds, then thunder
Awakens the spirit hidden away long before the journey began.
Just before I reach the ground, I pull up
And graze lightening-sharpened treetops.
From below comes the warning songs of birds,
The roar of cats red in tooth and claw,
And howls of great ages making out brutal kingdoms.
I slow my flight and stand upon the tallest leaf
And wonder why I ever feared the jungle.

— THE WAY IS NOT —

The Way is not the Way it's not
Give me all your good words;
I have none of my own.
Give me all your hearts and screaming cheese and welly wells.
Give me all your yesterdays and save your
Tomorrows for a rainy day.

I have no need for the Other right about now.
Write about then.
Freeze time in a screen shot,
Live a life that smiled with a girl's face;
Bring her back so the rest of us can see
What she saw in the Way you had
Touched Joey's face.

Just for once,
Let the Way that can be written,
Be enough.

— TAKE YOUR ANGER AND TURN IT —

raging
your sense of self
seething
don't follow the examples around you
there will be other worlds
where spirit and creation,
hatred and negation, taken flight, can be your messengers
pathfinders
can carry your invitation into forever unfolding tales
these worlds are not found by escaping through intricately carved doors
opened with hard-earned keys
they are the doors
you are the landscape, you are the plot
you are all the characters
heroes, villains, witches, demons, child messiahs, jaded lovers, whore,
      whoremongers
comedy relief
and you are the denouement
the worlds you pass through are your instruments

play them for all they're worth
kill them, if you please
kiss them, and make them whole
discard them, or give
them as a parting gift
to me.

— LESSONS FROM SCHOOL OF HUMAN WASTE —

From Avalon to Zanzibar, the Blue Sea lovers played,
And not a tipsy surfer girl was seen without a smile.
But melted into multitudes where not a step I stayed;
Yet molding concrete mem'ry, I watched them all a while.

From walks of life I'd not yet dreamed and places I'd never go;
The hotter the sand, the cooler the shades, the darker the skin would glow.
When money changed hands, the sins were forgiven; but never forgotten,
    you know,
The tide was high, and so was I, but the sun was sinking low.

Plans were laid, false friendships made; the parties stumbled on,
At San Jose, we fought the law, and lost past old San Juan.
We fried and dove Bonita Cove; discovering Mission Bay,
But the great Coronado fell. We gave up the following day.

Beach bums are a darkening shade of strange, even while young.
They're a little like cats, yet live like rats; and sharper with the tongue.
Come fall, they all just fade away; leaving me high and dry.
So came and went another short life, and not a single goodbye.

I see that soon, I'll relive a past I simply cannot lose;
The home that's closest to my heart, the friends I know and trust,
I'm going back to nurse my soul and pay back all my dues;
But after my wakening spirit is healed; it's mean, cruel world or bust!

— UNTITLED —

Mountain on mountain,
The drumbeats of the Earth
Heard in love-dreams
In axed woods
In dive bars on the edge of town.

— CALCULUS OF DECEPTION —

Underdetermined love, overdamped spirit;
Category errors make for charmed bedfellows.
How can one plus one equal everything?
Contradictions fill nothing but an empty set
Of words, of sleeping beside a stranger
Known since before eyes were more than eyes,
Of secret victories shared and failures traded with you and
Who you said you were,
Of endings that weren't.

Some pain is asymptotic, never quite reaching zero.
Some is only conjectured, never proven,
Dipping and diving just beyond the critical line.
My pain is elliptic, doubly periodic;
It defies elementary deconstruction.
It makes circles into squares and
Fills the complex plane with distortions of you.
It lingers in essential singularities,
It bleeds infinite residues,
It drags the frame.

— LOST AT SEA —

very the sail, the billowed sail that brought me here
in tatters, soaking, whips the wind
very the sun, the searching sun, which led the way
behind gray mountains hides.

bring the seabirds
wings tilted and swaying,
low between the spray, high over torn sail
let them cut these stays
take the frayed ends
and lead me home.

— LAST REQUEST —

Will you when endings show
The last of three is not me
Will you forward my dreams

To a name and a soul
Neither of us knows?

Who was she, you never said
So never asked so never forgotten
Nor need for forgiveness
For what she gave
I was too washed out to offer.

But I know she's gone.
The day your eyes dropped
From mine and mirrored both
Both of us spoke only of the day
And in the night you wept.
Walked out into the trees but I heard.
The trees wept as well.

And when you are left
For my shell has never been filled
Even once, though we smile at the same skies
Oh, when you are left
Which name will you speak?
Speak neither, but find one more.
You, who burn with every new star seen
Burn again, for fire in this life lights
More than sticks and storied faces
Light a new heart and another until
Every corner of the night sky smiles back.

— UNQUIET SPRING —

scooping up what's left of life
down by the seaside
scooping wings and flippers and tossing another dead crab
into the bucket of filth
into the catcher of capitalist dreams
into the net of our million-mile-long extension cord
wringing necks, drenching octopuses in our Louisiana sweet crude
wreaths for the dying,
dying earth

— UNTITLED —

fairy floating by
on a errand of
get it while you can
because face-to-face still beats
half-written glimpses through flatscreen windows
edited, spell-checked, filtered from the prying eyes of
third party nobodies
intruding on friends who don't need passwords
a few hours of
say nothing
because talking matters.

— LOVE IN THE TIME OF LONELINESS —

The first night I met her,
I slept beside her;
Whose lips were an inch from my own.
I knew only the shape of her body
And that all her life she had been alone.
She gave me as game
A number and name.
She'd made for herself on the way to the ball.
She gave me as trust,
Her life and her lust
But gave me no more reason to call.

The first night I met her,
I saw the pain in her eyes;
Whose smile was the face of my soul.
I knew only the sound of her sleeping
And I'll hear it long after she reaches her goal.
When with a last bite
Her clock catches midnight
She promises me that I'll never know,
But, with her first gentle kiss
And the jewel of her kindness,
She found the one place that death cannot go.

— LEGAL LIES —

Inhale the truth;
Enhance your mind's eye;
Feel the fullness;
You'll never die.

Smoke the peace pipe;
Reach for the stars;
Know what is out there
Is already yours.

The rhythm of religions speaks with a spark!
Unfolding fantasies dance in the dark,
Archaic, ancient, making their mark,
While the radiant redhead plays in the park.
Can it be that simple?
Really work out that well?
Give yourself up to the visions unveiled,
The drifting gray door;
Finding your secret identity will set you free
And maybe more.

Why ask why?
Doesn't it sell?
Feeling the patterns and peeling them back;
Whetting your appetite and getting the knack.
Needing a single and feeding the pack;
Flaunting your fortune but wanting a snack.
This bud's for you,
Or can't you tell?

— UNFORGOTTEN THOUGHTS —

Well, Heather, I see you're not home again.
I don't know if you're just too busy or what,
But the next call will have to be yours,
'Cause I don't like talking to answering machines,
When the message is never returned.

— WINSTON SMITH —

Quotes of dead poets embrace the legs of lonely high school girl blogs
Dancing smileys renamed emotions because this isn't your granddaddy's
    internet.
Dancing participles cause epic flamewars that bring the downfall of mods in
    a community of pet lovers.
Wii are the dead
Wii are the dead
Wii are falling into chaos surrounding a singular flat earth
Wii are keying immortal nothings into ears of bored NSA employees
Wii are wearing fluffy house shoes and pajama bottoms and wife beater T
    shirts and raccoon heads stolen from football mascots
Wii are not touching lips to lips, fingers to cheeks, ankles to thighs
Wii are waiting for someone to tell us when real life begins
Wii are altogether all the time if we want it; but
Wii are all alone anyway.
Wii are the dead.
Wii are the dead.
U r the dead.

— INSIDE/OUTSIDE —

She smiles as she flicks
Her subtle destroyer
But she loses her cherry instead
Which falls to the floor
As broken ashes
And dying embers.
    WHY DID THEY DO IT?

Conversation turns
From sex to a darker shade of sex
The physics to the philosophy
The end to the beginning
To the end.
    WHY'D THEY PUT THEIR FAITH TO THE FLAME?

Far from our words are our lofty dreams
And far from our paths is ever-after

As far from the sounds is a song
And far from the song, the singer.
    WHY BRING DOWN THE HIGHEST HOPES?

Another smile for a lock of gold
Brushed beside a verdant eye
And a wispy puff of smoke.
    WHY SACRIFICE THE CHILDREN?

From politics, to pubic hairs
From here to eternity.
    WHY THE CALL TO ARMS?

We all listen to a little, lost child.
    WHY DIE?
    WHY?

— THERE WILL BE SAD SONGS —

Ways of knowing your innermost
Laughing at misunderstood jokes
Calling just to say
Forgotten names paired with faces belonging to
Vanished children
On the edge of seventeen.

Asking your forgiveness for
Falling in the spring, springing into fall
Well-trained voices speaking recklessness
A lock of hair pushed aside evergreen eyes
Doesn't bother me. Does your conscience bother you?

Work-weary and worn down
Downy pillows in pristine hotel penthouses
Snuggling in the sleeping bag on a mountain morning
Recalling all your best days, and my worst
It's bound to be better than
Goodbye.

— THREE WAYS TAKEN —

Some are called.
Voices are first heard in anger
Replayed between sobs
An end to it all
Whispered by unseen friends
Shouted over glaring red and blue
Accompanied by laughter
By slaughter
Of the soul—

Some are beaten
Down by fate
The most loving
Drafted into the ranks
By physician's words
By heartfelt prayers
By last rites
Given before that first pain felt
Of the war within.

Some sing out
Every moment of every day
The child unworldly
Seen only in passing
Skipping across mountain peaks
Without a goodbye
Cut.

— JUDAS KISS AND THE LAYING ON OF HANDS —

Death traps
all great loves
in the moment when
a kiss on
what once was a child's cheek
becomes the proof of resurrection

until,
after a hundred summer nights' lifetimes,

ginger snaps
up every fine thing
with only a word
of intimacy and tender touches
remembered after all the pain
the kisses could not cure.

— CONTRADICTION —

Since when did the burning
                         soothe?
Going on, I don't know
                  how many years?
Since we saw each
                otherwise, how could we have known?
How could we have seen beyond each other's eyes if we'd never
                                       strangled what was for us
All that was
       for us
             all that was
                 all, that is
For us no more
       than fingers pulled back from a hot skillet's handle;
No more than scratches on my back
                   I can't see
Don't even know if you left
               scars, yet, running my fingers over them,
I can still feel the warmth of blood.
                  I can still hear the softness of your voice,
Searing my soul to ashes. Since when did the soothing
                             burn?

— BARBEQUE AND THE BOYS ARE BACK AGAIN —

Once, upon a hot tin roof
Two tabbies tore into an almost-human hate.
Fur fly, don't bother me;
I've got higher thoughts to snack on.
Cats . . . cats . . .
Fort Worth Cats, baseball bats, backwards caps, capslock brats.
Forget the feline furor, it's trenchcoat time.
Break on through, baby,
The end is coming, and it's asking for you.
It knows, you see. It sees the bee in your bonnet, the bats in your belfry, the
    ghost in your
Kitty litter tossed over oil spills; smells like frying pan french fries
French maid outfits on Japanese schoolgirl uniforms on cheerleader skirts
    on forty year old
Men on sports; boys of summer; girls of the southwest conference
Grinding, grilling, gritting teeth while the wives lounge on plastic
Swimming pool sweat shirt tail wagging pants slapping laughter
Dogs in the backyard; cats fighting on high
Who's watching the kids?
Are in the basement
Cooking up their own brew
Here, in the sleepy town
Of Columbine.

— DARKNESS IS ME —

Once, walking was me, and mountains bowed themselves beneath my feet.
Once, kissing was me, and hearts beat faster beneath my hands.
Once, dreaming was me, and the most secret worlds unveiled themselves
    before my eyes.
Then, the slow darkening came and brought with it mistresses of the quick
    claw and deafening beauty.
Walking became the law, and now I'm the rogue.
Kissing became the projectiles, and now I'm the battered wall.
Dreaming became the magician, and now I'm cut in half.

When walking was me, laughing was what held up dragonflies.
Growing was what children did while their parents weren't looking.
Dogs also laughed, and so did my oak tree; and even Green Herself
Let a smile cross Her face when walking through the forest
Was me.

When kissing the backs of hands was my garden gate
And kissing skinned knees was my embrace,
Names were given for playful goosebumps,
Crowns were lowered over the smooth foreheads of quiet mornings,
And the color that can only be seen in an emerald held by candlelight
Somehow found its way into Her eyes when kissing warm shoulders
Was me.

When dreaming won trials by ordeal was my classroom window
And dreaming lost in the forbidden desert was my morning ride,
Whole weeks of Summer were swallowed by tadpoles in the park.
Eyes blinked in the sky above campfires, and meadows danced, and caverns
    spoke in French;
And even that wise, old river tiptoed at the wedding of Green and Her
    Summer
While walking the primrose path held the ring.
Kissing the bride held the breath of the guests,
And dreaming happily ever after carried her over the threshold
Was me.

Very like the tide's undertow came the slow darkness.
The todash, the beast waiting beside the scales, last and lasting.
He made me smile at first, as questions often do.
He made Her turn away, though, and Her Summer winds blue.
It wasn't until Her tears cried out their own memory of pain
That I realized the darkness was dreaming before it was me.
Before the world's spine was crossed by the walking,

And before the kissing had learned how to sing,
She had known the touch of the dreaming, for it had bewitched Her.
The King of Broken Mirrors, whose name meant to steal
The frost on the blade that burned Her wrist.
The stone held in the right hand of God.

Summer fled, and, screaming, She followed.
Walking became the distant horizon
Where kissing drew up and leaped;
The wedding guests fell from the trees and turned to dust before their color
    could change;
Then dreaming peeled away from my shin as if flayed by a scythe
And returned to the back of the hypnotist.
So the darkness showed his true self.

Walking is never an infant, nor a crone without jewels.
Kissing is always a poet, or at least the drunken memory of one.
But dreaming is whoever it wishes to be, and has no shame or scruple.

Once, dreaming was me, and Happiness lived in my arms for a day and a
    night.
Green was Her eyes, Her voice, and Her name.
Once, dreaming was walking was kissing was me,
And I thought the three were the same;
But dreaming is everyone is no one is nothing
But he who pulls down the veil
To blind himself in the full light of Summer
So he won't see that he only lives
In the slow darkness.

― *Part Three* ―

Pop Corn Box

— CREATIVITY ONE —

With hands gifted and vision clear,
This girl whose views I hold so dear
Brings to life her deepest dreams
And makes the form of truth appear.
Pigments swirl from a seasoned brush;
Another unsung success.
Don't say that it's a masterpiece;
Her selfless heart assumes it's less.
Colors mingle in motley mixtures
As subconscious creatures secretly creep,
Fingers smear the saucy sculptures
And decipher descriptions as concoctions seep.
Never quite knowing what warrants await
In the finished tableau.
This girl, an unselfishly sensitive soul,
Might not see as much as you.

With tender touch and steady strength
Her hands possess serenity.
The moves they make and the charms they cast
Reveal her subtle mastery.
Impressionist artistry seems sufficient;
It needs no illicit inhibitions.
Her earnest expression proves most proficient
When accomplished without refined recognition.
Restricting rules and damaging discipline
Betray the free simplicity.
Inherent within her art's creation
That leads to its lovely symmetry.

How lucky are we who can sympathize
With such a wonder, a joyful surprise.
The girl who can happily illustrate
The beauty she witnesses with her bright eyes.
Thank you for the chance to see
The genius of your artistry,
And trust in the possibility
In all of us, you give to me.

— HUMAN NATURE —

Witches sing wooden symphonies; the nature of the world.
An evil man breeds robots to follow him whence he's hurled.
But what of the lowly hippie, the one with long hair curled?
He's beaten, jailed, and ridiculed once Old Glory is unfurled.

Holy fathers descending fall upon their word.
Machines are built for ending; the message isn't heard.
But where's the lowly hippie, the one you've named Absurd?
He's safely silenced in prison; full relations intended and inferred.

The soldier lives a death of hate; his time, a wasted lease.
Politicians speak with two tongues; while their salaries increase.
But what of the lowly hippie; the one who speaks of peace?
He's dreaming of fine green paradise, and waiting for the wars to cease.

— AFTER ALL —

Novel approach to an old problem
Kiss the girl whether you like her or not.
Life's too short
To stalk who you only think is the Perfect Other.
Ugly girls need love too.
Ugly boys for that matter,
And don't you know it.
So, kiss her.
Who will it hurt,
If by kissing
You get a little tongue
And, maybe a little play
And just maybe the beginnings of the thought
That maybe she isn't so bad
After all.

— CROOKED LINES —

Oh, what a hollahoops!
Searing stagefright farsight
Echoechoecho.

Encroaching cockroaches courting caravans of corndogs.
Sweet, I told ya. You know it's not time yet.
Force forgotten embargo beckons
Echoechoecho.

Diddly squat squash peddlers pound the pud.
Pouring and paying, they're puking and praying.
Sing, crotchrockets, sing. Hacienda honey intones, "Enough!"
Es no problemo, me amas, Soy el mejar.
Echoechoecho.

For gauche guerrillos au gratin
Sinking sideways into Southside.
I'd given your life.
Almost.
Echoechoecho.

Atchoo! And you and you and you.

— FRENCH VANILLA AND OLD PAPER —

Wednesday night the lights went out; the TV stopped spinning
Verbal abuse and the fuzz box #9 hid away from
The storm. All I had left were candles and a book
I've read many times before.

I got to wondering as the shadows danced around
Words I've known since well before high school
That this is what reading was for six thousand years before
The disingenuous battle between fluorescence and
Incandescence. This is how forbidden manuscripts
Were copied in the darkest years, how fathers
And the ghosts looking over their shoulders
Captivated children when parchment came at
A premium and security was measured in
Ink. This fairy flame and its faint scent of
French vanilla and old paper.

Sometimes I wish the lights would never come back on.

— NIBBLES —

Nibbles, come in from the cold
And huddle with us
By the hearth of good feelings.
Don't mind my callous and cannibal words
My heart is not my own
And lashes out when lonely.

You shine juicily for the moths.
All but one with clipped wings
Circle endlessly
Until your light and life alone
Burns your pedestal to the ground
And brings you to me.

I glide lazy uplifts
Of slow, friendly suicide.
The words just flakes of steel
Severed from a gilded edge
Sharpened on the wheel of morning.
I share with you a name.

Nibbles, don't consume yourself
Before you know the price
A self-inflicted hate exacts
From your banged and bleeding head.
Fickle friends and hopeful humps
May be full of sound advice,
But if you hear their words and not their wishes
You're already dead.

I am not above the call
Of the mighty god testosterone
And I cannot pull out the tongue
That knows no morals but its own,
So listen not to me.

— THE BEAST —

The prey of the beast screams bloody murder.
The line is so fine between hoping and hurting.

Hundreds of believers that pray for release,
As love looking down on them smiles and picks his teeth.
Trapped between heaven and hell,
He knows all the secrets you don't want to tell.
There's nowhere to run and there's nowhere to hide.
Love knows you all too well; he will find you.

Love is the ghost haunting your head;
Love is the killer you thought was your friend;
Love is the creature who lives in the dark,
Sneaking up, will stick you and painfully pick you apart.

Love is the poet, love sings the songs
Pointing his finger, you follow along.
Voices are calling, the master wants all of you,
Finding you, implores you to try and to fall.

Love is the leech sucking you dry;
Love is the vampire drunk on your blood;
Love is the beast that will tear out your heart,
Hungrily lick it and painfully pick it apart.

Love is the beast that will tear out your heart,
Hungrily lick it and painfully pick it apart.

Love is the killer you thought was your friend;
Love is the creature who lives in the dark,
Sneaking up, will stick you, and painfully pick you apart.

— CUBE: 7X7X7 —

A handful of plastic
six colors for six faces
intricate inner parts
only a few turns give more combinations
than all the particles in the universe
solved in ten minutes.

— WE'RE GOING BACK TO THE MOON —

I feel tea leaf fortune
Grace over fire fly blooming sky
Silly Sally Callie Marie watching waiting wondering
Fall back spring forward hold release reprise replay carrie white
Thrill kill blue oyster the band of the right hand of the grand old party
    favors
Which witch wicca wot angkor bangor maine refrain insane again
Gore Vidal rebel call wherewhithal all consuming
We're going back to the moon
Not a minute too soon

—'SCUSE, PLEASE MR. 'SPEARE! —

Taunting, tempting, tantalizing; delicacies abound;
But fly away as soon as day, and nowhere can be found.
Dark ones down below; just a bit too slow.
A loner I, but cannot cry, for who would hear the sound?

Wishing, walking, wandering, the forest answer's not.
No voice but fear that I can hear; no cry but my own thought.
I see them show their teeth; a warning from beneath.
The sun sinks low; a sad rainbow; and again come sprites I sought.

Hinting, hiding, holding; outward signs of praise.
But like before, they flee once more; come first the golden rays.
By the pricking of my thumbs; something wicked this way comes.
The end is near; alone I fear; for fairy nights and endless days.

Ghastly, grimly, gusting; the storm's at hand at last.
Weary eyes see the thrashing trees; deafened ears feel fiery blast.
The earth begins to drum; they know their time has come.
A last great sigh from the clouds thrown high; our world has finally passed.

— TALKING HEADS AND MOUTH BREATHERS —

Backsliding in the foreground
Ghosting lurking smirking surfing
Couch surfing with remote in hand
Framed by gold filigreed barristers
Barring all possible recriminations

Obfuscations
Justifications of cannibal nations
Rational factions nevertheless putting babies in tractions
Warring whoring boring
For oil and other poisonous foils
Conjunction function
What's your major malfunction?
There's no cure for the summer time news.

— VALENTINE —

Wishing, Wanting, Wondering,
We feel the love but miss
The high and tender gentleness
Within another's kiss.
Alone in a Lover's Holiday,
A tear can give our pains away.
Hurting, hiding, handling
Our past with failing skill,
We give in again to mindless fears
As we know we always will.
Falling at first glance,
We never really had a chance.

— UNTITLED —

Alone in love,
If not in life,
I read the faces of the crowd
To find the truth behind their eyes,
The love they hold within their shroud.

Some are lost
Inside the day
And shade the brightness that gleams in the night,
But dark risers also fall by the way
And hide their pain-reddened eyes from my sight.

Nibbles, don't close your eyes
Like the merciful few
Who've forever shut themselves out from your gaze,
They may call to you
With innocent cries.

— AN OTHER —

Kindling fire of sapling green;
The smoke is sweet,
But stings the eyes.

Breathing life into steel and stone;
The lines are clean,
But chill the heart.

Drinking from the blood spring;
The drought is filling,
But the thirst grows.

The separate city;
By day, infernal combustion.
By night, the dead lights.
By candlelight,
Spectral baths of pocari sweat.
By cell phone, everything and everything and everything
Always a neighborhood away.

Stillness under glass, the beauty sleeps,
Dwarfs gather and carry her crystal cage
Down
      Their
           Hole

Where tears mingle with dreams
That pour from the blood spring.

— TAKEN AND GIVEN —

There's a hole in the world
Where once shone a smile.

Secret heart
Burning

I never saw her
Until words were spoken over her head.

I never lay beside her
Until she was written
Into the living journal.

I was never touched by her
Until her hands were crossed
Over her heart.

Sweet smile
Shining.

There's a soul in the sky
Where dreamers saw stars.

— UNTITLED —

For finders, the spoils.
For winners, only keepsakes.
It is in the making that true treasure is found.

— GRAVITY AND MOTION —

Love's a strange attractor
No matter how people try to get closer to it
They only find each other.
Toiling day and night to make ends meet,
They run in circles, within circles.
And, when they hit, it can be as soft as a train wreck,
Or, as hard as a leaf falling into a pond.
It can be a glancing blow,
A touch of hands and lips,
Then distance seen through rain-streaked glass.
It can be tight, like two trees grown together,
Their roots mingling deep underground.
Or, it can be only leaves brushing as limbs are thrashed in the storm.
Let ours be as a river flowing into the ocean.
Though one is serene, it's dense with the soil of a thousand miles.
Though the other is choppy, it can never run dry.
And, once together, no one can tell them apart.
Until they rise again into the sky.

— THE FLAME AND HER MOTH —

It's a race, she cried;
A much more lively soul than I.

With a hand to her lips, she tried to hold on to our first kiss
And the softest touch—only one!
Only once was all it took . . .
A kiss may destroy a philosophy.

(The SpanFrenAmgirl said.)

Smoke rings and strange things painted on the chrysalis
Looking for a flame to awaken the moth—
Was it me? Was it you? Was it just the thing to do?

Which way was home?

I can't go back! He cried;
And I know myself for the fool.

A finger's trace across a cheek hides an eye behind a strand
Of bitter memory.
Oh the harshest word, only once!
Only once, and all the tomorrows crowd together,
Grasping at words formed from the substance of that word.

(Unforgettable)

The smoke dissipates, but the flame still burning,
And no one to patch the wings.
Will it fly? Will it die? Will it ever know?

And who won?

— THE VOICE OF WAITING —

She is a secret age
When days go by between the sunrise
And midnight cries.
She lives in cotton and paper
Written in hands living and dead,

Flirting with tomorrows, watchers, moments.
Somewhere soars a heart on wings of stained lace,
But she knows him only by the brush of wind that holds him.
Together is a prophesy she reads on a leather-bound page;
Still, she looks up to the top shelves of her neighborhood book store,
Hoping at least to recall the author's name.
She would sing the color of autumn leaves, but soft
The sound of his shadow's passing makes her tremble again.
Waiting is not in the clouds with her sun-dazzled becoming;
Up there swing and spring only the self, the now, the here.
Waiting sleeps on her shoulder at night and crawls onto her breast in the
    morning.
Awake, it whispers, but not loudly enough.
And hollow thoughts come with the traffic,
And glaring, shiny nights pass under streetlight skies,
And all the dreams of her lunch break drowsing
Are drowned out by are you okay and conflicts
In the name of time clock friendship.
She is a shrinking, outside the world of vacation pictures and randomly
    filled bookcases;
She is only the growing when a silent sun, brushed aside her pillow by that
    faraway forgetful heart perched on delicacy,
Warms the place where waiting was, only two long breaths before.
Sometimes the hidden places of her room are larger than nations,
And populated by more yesterdays than faces.
Once she had glimpsed He Rides the Sky, the name of that day as lost as all
    the others,
She could only see blue through her bedroom window,
She could only dance to the sound of thunder,
She could only touch the night through cotton and paper,
She could only shed tears at the last hour, and
She could only hear the beating of butterfly wings,
Still louder than the voice of waiting.

— UNTITLED —

Save me from the slavery of a lonely heart.
Save me from the dreams of others.
I say this to you, but it is I who must find the truth.
I know you cannot give me the solace,
But you can quiet my screaming soul long enough
For me to seek it myself.

— CIVILIZATION 101 —

Domestic bliss is ignorance
Wal mart sells wife beaters by the pallet
I'm loving it
But no longer can spel
Let's go twitting
For the best of everything
Including the price of
Civilization 101

— AUTUMN LEAVES —
(Meaning Autumn leaves the area.)

She leaves no tracks in the moist earth;
She snaps no twigs nor rustles the autumn leaves.
Her breath is clear, despite the nearing frost;
The sound breaks the simple peace left behind by
Creatures now sleeping and
Winter winds still waiting to awaken.

Yet the land knows her.
Snowflakes harken to her thoughts and
Seal her dreams;
Pines, firs, and aspens bend to her passing
And moan at her wake.
Her beauty is no more in the living,
But the living see it.

She carries with her no reminder of summer,
She sheds no tears.

Finally, after all earth-bound voices are stilled
She takes a last walk to the clearing
Above Bird Woman Falls,
Waiting for the silvery night after the first snow
When the stars will come to lift her up
To hear the song that the moon sings.

Saying farewell to her last few friends,
She turns her eyes to the sky and smiles,
And the wolves cry.

— THE GIFT —

boxes of holiday joy
carefully cushioned
by foam peanuts and obsolete periodical media
formerly known as newspapers
bring a seemingly rare look of wonder to the eyes of children
now hidden by dark circles and crow's feet.
watch how they grin as the bows fall
tear off the falling wrap
and tease away the strip of tape
until all that's left is the gift of remembering
what it was like
when Christmas was enough.

— DON'T FROM WAITING —

don't from waiting
lose the will
justification sought after
when the purpose dies by
second guesses
just do it.

see in yourself
not the thing finished
not the thing begun
but the thing becoming.

don't from getting ready
forget to be
gathering the right tools in
fear in the name of
preparation
just do it.

— LITTLE MISS DISCORD —

Safety pins through earlobes;
Are these what allow kids to hear
Comfort in the harshest dissonance?

Poetry slammed
Against the walls
Of your head
Not like mine.

Give me the count, Mr. Zildjian!
One step from standing to starting,
Two hearts beating the path,
Three choices making the crossroad,
Four winds whipping the sails the flags the leaves the outstretched hands.

Through the door came a little old woman.
She couldn't hear the music, no matter how loud.
She couldn't hear the verses, no matter how profound.
She could see neither the dancers nor the mildly amused audience.
Oh, but she was smiling, because she felt the wind.

Come away, my children,
The woman cried.
Leave the drowning place the crowded place the coward's place
And learn to dance as I do.

All backs were turned to her; all ears attuned to the stage
Where the whirling mixed the names of the muses,
Where colors flew from brass and wind and wire,
Where all senses were blinded but one.
Oh, but she was smiling, because she felt the wind.

Enjoy it, then, my children!
The woman laughed.
Let the furies display their masks for you for a night for the blindness is
				yours
Until you learn to dance as I do.

Bring it back, Mr. Majestic! Four walls to hold them,
Three fates befalling,

Two hearts in every beat,
One minute till midnight.

Sweat-streaked cheeks;
And steel safety slips free
From ringing ears
But not these.

Violent verse and prose passion
Change to surprised whispers
When the last is called,
Fall to awed silence when heads begin to turn
To see the woman smiling
As she dances to the wind in the door.

— THERE IS NO PLACE —

There is no place which love calls home;
Love calls all places yesterday.
Run to yesterday and you find strangers laughing
For forgotten reasons.
Friends speaking with no voice.
Tears falling from faceless others
You once knew better than yourself.
There is no place because
There is only here
For love
When love is a touch.
There is only there
For longing in love
When touching is yesterday;
Here and there move with the touch;
Leave when parting is sweet sorrow
But clings to no known place;
Here and there are together and apart
Are we and we once were.
Look in the empty room,
The misty mountainside
And a thousand hidden heavens;
Love remembers those, but
Calls home only
The here and the now.

— CHANGING IN THE CAR —

walking backwards, leaving elaine in the field alone
seeking out the words
while the witch in witchita falls . . .
the one whose little path would make me sad.

weary, weary traveler
let the song drown out your sorrows
let the breeze bring chills
let the dappled green sun flow.

climb the fence, books and pens
take a look at the sky, just before you die
within the darkest wood, elaine still waits
in the field alone.

— CIRCLING —

We reach, but the ring swings free;
You have to get off the carousel to catch it.
Once left behind, though,
The horses no longer jump and prance,
Bob and dance.

Entered by morning, the carnival smells of popcorn and cotton candy
But, after night falls,
The dizzying lights blind.
When the cryers call closing,
All the little children have already gone,
Having ridden away with the horses.

— UNTITLED —

A fortune is not found in the Seven-Elevens,
But the corner booths in greasy-spoons.
It is not written on cards,
But can be read.
The future is not found by the reading,
But in the power of the words.
It is not written on stone,
But it can be broken.

Your fate cannot be found in you,
But in the faces of others.
It is not for you to see,
But it can be found.

— MARY —

Be calm,
Mary.
You've nothing to fear;
The problems of the worlds
Can't touch you here
In your heart.

You are protected;
It is filled
With pain resurrected
With Love.

Be still,
Mary.
You've done much more
Then we should ask.
Today's work is done;
Dream your silent dreams.

You've finished more
Than we have started;
You're one to our many;
You've filled us all.

Be patient,
Mary.
You've prepared the way
Into Life;
Whoever waits, knows
You're born blessed.

You're living Loved.
You're working Rewarded.
You're waiting Fulfilled.
Your prayers Answered.

— UNITY —

Warm was the sunrise, and Cara danced;
Golden hair spinning.
For who can sleep beyond the break
With love beginning?

Felis fought imagined foes in the hay.
Trog just stumbled through a doze of lazy play.
Krylon slept with fitful dreams, Unity at his door.
Mando snored between the beams, Ollie on the floor.

Cara jumped and swung and whirled, her lover on her mind;
Once again with calm delight, she left the world behind.

Bright was the morning, but Andy wept;
Blue eyes burning.
For nothing could bring her father back
Or the world from turning.

The cat stalked a noisy bird, down by the creek;
But stopped and tormented the ape, instead, who'd snuck a peek.
The Wizard woke with quite a start; the guard just stood.
The chief, however, slumbered on; the boy wished he could.

Andy caught a glimpse of sun, and released another sigh;
Wishing dearly instead of him, that she herself had died.

Thoughts to himself, Venture wondered;
Forever endeavor;
Because God himself had commanded,
Until life and body sever.

Wakened from a foggy dream, Canon rose;
And strode again upon the grass.
Mind still full of imagined foes,
For only soldier thoughts he knows,
He walked indifferently past
His lovely, doting lass.

Cara blindly tumbled on;
Her heart entranced.

While none but Felis, and maybe Trog
Knew for whom she danced.

Andy finally found herself;
Alone, but alive.
The dawn had broken, and so her heart,
But somehow, she'd survive.

Krylon gathered at the fire, a wealth of earthy smells,
The food he stewed and the drink he brewed,
Seemed louder to Ollie's ears,
Then the Wizard's wake-up bells.

It's the taste of tenderness, and the sound
Of Unity awakening.

— UNTITLED —

Why, you ask, not to die?
A question that reason doesn't serve.
Suffice it to say, I love you;
Suffice it to say—a kiss instead
On your hand, on your cheek
On your tender lips—
I want you.

Loneliness is not fickle
And love is not a single word.
Suffice it to say, I love you;
Suffice it to say—can I have a hug?
A strong one, a solid one
A moment immeasurable—
I need you.

Why, indeed, not end the hatred
As home and hearth fall short of hope?
Suffice it to say, I love you;
Suffice it to say—talk to me
With your eyes, with your heart
With you tender lips—
I love you.

— UNTITLED —

Lovers carry contentment
Like a badge
Fighters carry triumph
Like a flag
Sages carry wisdom
Like a handful of propaganda
What can I carry
When I must walk on my hands?

— WITHOUT —

In the crackle-talk of radio
A morning without music
Until—
In the fragrance of oil and books
Harvard on the highway
Except—
In the days of disillusionment
A test of wills
Unless—
In the blink of an evergreen eye
A crazy little thing called
Without.

Music is the love of lunacy
Fixed in the camera's eye
Exposed in the mind
Of the beholder
The lunatic.

All together
Craving all community
Finding in all combinations
Players and all but lovers
Looking in all the wrong places.

In the darkest depths of hopelessness
A flimsy, fluttering heartbeat
Until—
In the sheltering arms of mortality

An end to it all
Except—
In the morning of abandonment
Another self undone
Unless—
In the blink of an evergreen eye
A crazy little thing called
Without.

— UNTITLED —

As the morning stage
Whimpers into afternoon
And all transport-endowed cast members
Go off and whistle a gassy tune,
A seemingly grateful I
Gives a few winks a try.

Oh . . . kay . . . here we go
Out of the platonic blues
Into a me with more Freudian hues,
A bouncy, beastly toy land
With my name on the sign; my head in the sand.

— NIBBLER —

In a room full of nicks
Your name should be Nibbler
Meek enough
Not to leave a mark
On sweaty backs
And across your naked heart.
Raven tangle
Crestfallen dreamsilk
A crown of encrusted rock
On a head bound to rolling thunder;
The lover you're under
The man child, the star.
In a room full of names,
Your name should be Nibbler.

— DISTRACTED BY YOU —

What's the square root of you?
I heard her ask
Distracted, you see, looking out the window.
Girls playing hopscotch.
I don't remember much more than that,
But still wonder
Why I was looking out
When she was sitting right there beside me.

I lost my hearse!
I heard her yell
Distracted again. Watching traffic while leaning into a turn.
A woman in a red, sleek something.
I can't tell you why the thought of red lips in a red car
Seemed so inviting,
When her arms were holding me so tightly.

Oh, God, Roger, just a little beeper!
I heard her gasp.
Distracted for the last time.
Sharing a lemonade at the food stand.
Polyester uniform, black tag, brown hair.
I shouldn't have let it bother me;
I shouldn't now, but it's only,
During these fleeting moments of clarity that I recall,
When your smile was meant for me.

— UNTITLED —

The love of life was lost to me
Much growing sight it smothers
And on this lonely road I know
There rarely have been others.

This is where you come in.

I met you not long ago,
And I think I saw, perchance,
A true daughter of the earth;
A soul where dragons dance.

We teach.

The soul is but an edge.
Reality, Illusion;
But when two hearts meet as one
They fall into confusion.

We touch.

I cannot say I love you,
For my soul's closed to me.
I bid you, answer for yourself,
For you can truly see.

Talk to me.

Tell me what you think of me.
Oh, please don't hide from me.
I see this trouble you've had yourself,
But you know that I'm not he.

The end result—
The joy of life replaced,
I can see in you
A soul where dragons danced.

— NEOMENIA —

One second in transit
The magic that is mirrored in your eyes.
Twenty-eight days.
Yet only the fullness is celebrated
By lovesick fools and backwards-looking dreamers.
There is magic in the darkest nights,
There is fullness in the cup overflowing,
And the wolves do not sing of love.

One second for the light
Of silent mountains and frozen seas
To reach behind your eyes,
And one second more
For the tear in mine to fall.

Such beauty . . .
Such beauty . . .

In the new moon.

— BETTER THAN MINE —

Should I go into another dream?
Lose myself in fantasy when being in the now is so important?
Do I even have a choice?

There wasn't one, but three.
The tall one, the one with long hair, and the one who called me dumb.
I kissed the one with long hair.
We shared home room, Terry and I.
Her eyes were warm and green,
A perfect pair to go with her soft voice.
Melted my heart. Told me I made her nervous
In a good way.
Said that she'd never let anyone see her poetry before.
Better than mine, that's for sure.

Her words; whispered in my ear in the backyard, whispered in spiral
        notebooks, whispered in the darkness of the park;
Touch me.
Her eyes; spring leaves at play in a northern wood.
Her hands; bringing life to the piano on stage after class, taking my breath
        after sundown on a school night.

Her words; receding, fading, hiding behind the years;
Touch me.

— MY WAY OR THE HIGHLIGHTER —

Straight flush right down the toilet of lost dreams; childhood screams for
        escape!
I love to use sentences that aren't quite sentences like that girl not the tall
        one!
It's a liberating feeling, really. You can start out on your back porch and go
Straight edge or French curve depending on mood.
There are no limits in the realm of English verse.
Well, any language, if you happen to grab it in the fullness.
Why stay between the lines, anyway?
Why, when it's so much more funicular at the Royal Gorge?
We couldn't go across the bridge that day, though, because of highlighting
        passages she loved in her favorite book.

I could be crazy enough to take you all the wayside by I-20 with David,
> Christi, Brenda, and Norris. We played Mario Bros with terrible
> hang gliders running off the cliffs overlooking Black's Beach.

It doesn't really have to make sensational sense machine closed down, but
> the building was still useful for making out on breaks or smoking
> jays at in-park partitions of unity are only guaranteed if the para
> compartners condition is satisfied.

See? You have no idea where I might go next door to help Val clean out her
> garage.

Don't let the grammar nazis fool you. There's more to writing thanatos,
> twin of hypnos, the personification of dealing straight flushes.

— POP CORN BOX —

Hot-buttered blood coursing through my veins;
The lion's leaping and no one at the reins.
At the crack of a whip, a gnashing of teeth;
And forgotten feelings well up from beneath
Omigod! I think I'm dead!
My heart has stopped—I'm seeing red.
The roar of the crowd is fading away;
A voice from my past has something to say.
Wasn't she fine? Yes, wasn't she right?
Where is she now?
Didn't she comfort you, fresh from the fight?
What of your vow?
Can't you even answer yourself?
Don't you know how?

Walking the high wire, knowing that I
Followed a firebird, living a lie.
Swallowing flames, and feeling them fry;
I earned the pain, so why did she die?
Against my will, I take a breath.
The stench, though heavy, is not one of death.
The one-eyed Jack's stopped calling me back,
So why is my mind still whispering 'Beth'?
Aren't I alive? Isn't this real?
The management frowns.
Have I really broken the seal?
Have I crossed out of bounds?
Or, is this just another part of the dream?
Send in the clowns!

— *Part Four* —

An Evening Ride

— MORNING RIDE —

It was a calm, dark, warm morning when I went riding. I rode through the park before the sun woke up, before the orchestra sang the dawn.
I rode on. Through the city, with its black, wet streets mirroring the signs and the dark, dark sky.
The rain had stopped, but a few clouds remained, flying swiftly across the stars. The air was still.
I rode on. The trail I was on was rough, but I felt like I was gliding through a dream world, a land with a life I could not touch.
Yet there was no life.
No movement.
No sound except my old black bike,
Nothing but the landscape around me.
I rode on. By the river, the deep, unmoving, jet black Trinity River.
Not a ripple.
Even the mist stood still, waiting.
It was a fairy land, a gentle reminder.
I rode on. The gargantuan buildings like sleeping giants to my right.
I was nearing the end.
Were they giants? Or merely metal and concrete tombs?
There was still no movement but my own.
I was not there. I was moving through this dream, but not in it.
The bridge. The stark, broken-down bridge. I crossed it.
I rode on. The cliff below the buildings, one path winding up.
I rode it. Through the trees and the monuments, I saw the buildings.
Civilization.

That did not hold my gaze for long.
I looked out, over the cliff, from the terrace jutting out like a tongue to taste the scene below.
I was just in time.
The sky was moving. Clouds left to right. Faster than I could ever ride.
The abandoned planet; the towering smokestacks; all was still.
Then it came.
That first sign of light.
Below it, miles away, streetlights gleamed.
A single ray burst forth; upward straight it shot.
It pierced the clouds.
Another.
Soon, they were joined by another glow, darkest crimson.
The sky lit like a candle.

The glow reached the moving clouds and ignited them, also.
A car drove down the road to the right.
The trees were brushed by the wind.
On the horizon the sun arose.
At first, a small sliver, then more and more until it was alone in the air.
The clouds melted away. Just like that.
The sun was bright and yellow, and hot.
There was a noise behind me. Downtown had awakened, along with the rest
    of the world.
I gave one last glimpse over the panorama. A miracle in Technicolor.
I rode on.

— PAGES —

I buy a book instilled with mystery;
I read, and escape the world around me.
I fall into an epic story,
Of magic and high fantasy.
But I can't leave you
Or deceive you.
My soul tries in vain to weave you
Into the song,
My lonely melody.
It would be wrong
To end your harmony—
Please forgive me.

Plots unfold;
Words astound;
Sentences written
By authors renowned.
A feeling of accomplishment.
The book is done; my brain is spent.
But you're still here
Awaiting me.
Oh, why did you stay,
So patiently?
Do you love me?
Oh, yes. I see!

— PURITY (UNTRUE) —

The simple beauty of a smile
From this young, enchanting one
Disarms the most perverted mind
And renders wicked thoughts undone
For who could dare betray the love
She freely gives to everyone?
When praised, she lowers her soft brown eyes
To presume is not her due.
When cursed, she answers without offense,
Instead, their acceptance she strives to renew.
But, when told three wonderful words
She softly says, "I love you, too."

The kindness in her merry face
Is shown to all she meets
And no matter their mood or prejudice
Always with words of cheer, she greets.
So fulfilled in life is she
She feels no foul conceits.
Through days of dull, menial work
And nights of uncertain release
She seeks her own resolved reform
So, forever does her goodness increase,
She dwells not on other's wrongs,
But, instead reveals her inner peace.

This girl of God rules emotions of many
Yet, treats her true friend without pity
To know her is to behold a miracle
Though her eyes may show silent denial
To understand why I love her so,
You need only to see her smile.
Pray that you might see her smile,
Thank you for her endless ways
You prove to me that life's worth living
And thank you for your inspiration
And revealing to me a love worth giving.

— THE OUTDOOR LIFE —

Very weak now, holding on by fingernails . . .

Dropping backwards, I catch a glimpse of
Havasu Falls and Turner Falls and Upper Yosemite and Bird Woman and
Training days at Six Flags, going down Splashwater Fa . . .
Ten Thousand tons of helo carrier in San Diego Bay, North Island
Rocking gently in the warm breeze under a harsh Texas sun
Setting up camp downtown for tickets to the twenty-two years late Star
      Wars movie
Moving step by step past Knoxville because my dad won't go between the
      crawling lanes ahead
Behind Jennifer in Mrs. Carter's class because I get to see her scratch her
      neck
While walking across the mighty Mississippi on pebbles, Lake Itasca
New York, though I can only see the buildings through the gray
Rain clouds roiling above and my motorcycle isn't going any faster.
Jumping from the roof so the cops won't get me
Teeth gritty from all the sand and where are the dinosaur
Bones

    Crumble

        Blood

            Flows

                Heart

                    Stop

— THE GHOST OF LOCKRIDGE MANOR —

A fistful of friends—
Leaning on shoulders,
Learning old secrets,
Living and searching,

And laughing at fates
That will surely find them
Bored in the morning.

And I in the corner—
Fishing the shadows
For signs and serenity
And falling through selfishness
As thoughts of my fellows
Lose way to fond feelings
Of longing for you.

Rising gray tendrils of miniature dragon-breath
Lead me from this place and waken my mind
To the truth of my loneliness
And wishes for a healing kiss
To place on your tender lips for your kindness in kind.
I see through the smoke's billow
Soft hair on your pillow
A fire in my eyes though my heart becomes blind—
A fire as the dragon stick
Held at my fingertips—
A small borrowed candlestick all the warmth I can find.

Unspoken acceptance and reluctant farewells—
Accompany the dawn as a fellowship ends
Where once was air dance
With smoke and nonsense,
Now there's cool silence and an absence of friends
As alone left I
For no job to apply
Or no knowledge of why upon that all depends,
So again my heart falls
Outside these cold walls
And timidly calls out the message it sends.

— UNTITLED —

When walking upon the shore
Of a sea, hidden in mountainsides,
Tread lightly, for dragons have also left footprints there.
If you swim the grand rivers
Between worlds out of time
And feel yourself intruders;
Smile, for the destructive waters themselves
Brought you here, well below the present.
Hold in your mortal hands an ancient life,
One spared of violence for you to wonder at.
As I wonder.
Raise your eyes to the shriek of the wings of the canyon
And see yourself from his back;
But look instead to the playful mice,
Who present eagles prey.

— UNTITLED —

A hushed voice and a tender touch
Diffuse the fog in my waking mind,
While a glimpse of autumn and auburn hair
Hints of a dawn outshined.
The freckle faced girl with a burden to bare—
And not an unkind word.

Though slight of hand and less of time,
She proves a golden life begun;
And when I'm held in darkened thrall
She shows me the sun.
Who can answer the highest call?
I know she's the one.

For she is a survivor
Of a past and a pain
Only few can know
And through it grow

Or slowly go insane.
A yearning soul and a furtive heart
Show by, in her shy pursuit
Of yet another uncaring lover
An emptiness absolute,
And to those informed, uncover
A girl who's more than cute.

— UNTITLED —

I have found something that travels faster than light.
That is my thoughts.
I can think of events before they may happen so as to be the cause or
 prevention of them.
I can think of motivation before I move.
I can tell the movement of objects before they affect me.
I can gage the position, if not the motivation, of other people before they
 appear.
I live at a certain speed.
No other objects or people move or live at the same unless by lack of
 distance between them and me.
The closer someone is to me, the closer in speed our minds are working.
Certain distances can be thought of as psychological in nature.
There is an intimate distance.

— LOGAN THREE —

Run, runner!
Time's wasting, and the carousel awaits,
What, at twenty-two can interest you
When twenty-one is a no-win dead-end?
Forces fed fantasies from birth
Birthed for the machine messiah
Boxed and caged and caught in the net.
You can find freedom in the Cathedral
Or, fly beyond the sky,
To Sanctuary!

— MIDNIGHT SUN —

There is a light
Clear and fresh and warm as day;
Makes the bright stars
Melt away
By comparison.

There's a thin, silver strand,
The lining of the forgotten cloud;
But rips across the dark sky
Electrically endowed
And touches all.

Here's the silent dreamer,
The fruit of the Tree of Knowledge;
When held close yields much more
Then marital pledge,
Yet vows her very life.

Where's the fatal stinger,
When death doesn't end your life;
When waiting is given you
Together forever your wife,
In the evening?

There is a Light,
The Purpose and the Way;
The deepest peace;
A word no one can say
Until the End.

— BEAUTY —

In the heat of a Monday morning sun,
I drank a coke with an old, close friend.
We spoke of the endless pursuit of fun
And how we'd spent the past weekend.
With dark sunglasses and faltering step
That he had partied was easy to see;
But when asked what wonder had caused my pep,
I said only, 'Susan Marie.'

The bewildering, beautiful Susan Marie.
'Isn't she the one who doesn't wear make-up?'
Right.

Between every addictive and dalliant vice,
Our conversation leapt to and fro;
But even when speaking of virgin sacrifice,
My mind flew over the rainbow.
Again and again my confidant crowed,
About his own latest affair,
And again and again he asked why I showed
Such attention to a girl with no cosmetic flair.
So little he knows of her beauty so rare.
'I wish you'd tell me what you see in her.'
Alright.

It's not that she won't take the care to appeal;
She just doesn't need all that paint to show grace.
The rouge in her cheeks from humilities real
And the glow that she gets from her love is her base.
Her lashes don't need to be lengthened by fraud;
Nor her lips to be reddened by stain from a case.
No make-up is cracked by that smile sent from God,
And around her soft eyes only laughter has a place.
No mask could add to her heavenly face.
'Oh.'

Thank you for setting an example for me,
Even though others may scorn your reserve,
And, thank you for the chance to enjoy your desire,
And to see the celebration you so richly deserve.

— UNTITLED —

Time willing, I would tell you all my tales;
But someone else is always on the stage,
And your eyes are always with him.
Faith willing, I could go on speaking anyway;
And hope someone else may be listening,
But my eyes are always with you.

— UNTITLED —

My mind is not in the gutter, for that's not where I would lay you,
But in a grand featherbed of fine satin and lace
With red roses and pink pillows
And a curtained canopy to shut out the sunrise
And the harsh voices of your family
And all the men who don't understand
When to just hold you.
And above us not a mirror
(For I don't need one to see what I would rather touch and taste),
But a silk tapestry of a crimson dragon in flight
With Ozzy eyes and wings filled with music
To sweep us off the earth and breathe fire into the night,
Into the morning, into sheltered beams of a well-earned sleep.

Where you see little I see the love, warm and unfamiliar,
Flowing freely to his children in arm and soul and yet to come;
A hallowed place where beats a lonely heart softly enough to hold a
    butterfly
Yet strong enough to say goodbye to a life too young to lose
And live on to wait and want and wish for one to begin anew.

On your lips alone my dreams have placed a thousand kisses
Soft and sultry, happy and hungry,
One for every moment of every day and every way
To say I love you without words.
If mood permits that my kisses should wander;
Let them caress you from temple to toe,
From freckle to freckle and cheek to cheek,
From curve of breast to small of back,
From heaven above to more-so below.

— SEDUCTION —

Sit here with me.
Do you see off to the side of the Dipper?

Don't laugh! I know it's cloudy.
Look inside, from that place where you've seen clear nights. In the
 mountains?
By the softly roiling sea?
Can you see It? Is It sparkling?
That's your star. I give it to you.
You're laughing again.
Of course, I don't own the stars, but that doesn't mean I can't give them to
 you.
Look closer now.
See the bluest dot among the sparkle?
That's where we're going to spend the rest of our lives.
It's a world without car alarms, or oil spills, or even garbage cans.
Ah, only a smile this time?
Just when I was falling in love with your laugh.
You want to know how we'll get there?
Take a walk with me and I'll show you.
There's that laugh!
You don't believe me.
That's alright.
You didn't have to believe in your star to see it through the rain, did you?
You don't have to believe for me to take you there, either.
You only have to hold my hand and come with me.

— SCARY HALL —

I told her how we met the day
Seventh grade started and you got lost
Looking for homeroom.

I was alone and you were new and
We were two of a kind.
We shared the lock in gym class and sat together in the stands.
We did each other's homework in the scary hall where the shadows hid our
 hands.

Oh, Sherry, it was the '80s,

When love was on the radio and each sunrise meant I'd see your smile
    again.
Hold on, hold on.

I told her everything;
How the boys would run down the scary hall,
And throw pennies to distract us from each other.
How the girls would laugh about the parties where they kissed,
But only when the boys were there.

I was your secret love and you were my life,
Trading smiles between the pews in church.
We saved up our allowances to buy music for one another.
We met behind the trestle in the park, where the boys never played.
We traded Friday nights at each other's houses
And talked low on the phone so our parents couldn't hear.

It wasn't gross.
It wasn't selfish.
It wasn't sick.
It wasn't a sin.
But we hid every look behind our books
And every touch beneath our sheets
And every song that said I love you,
While other girls laughed.
Oh, Sherry, it was the `80s,
When holding hands meant everything and each sunset meant tears washing
    away in the creek.
Hold on, hold on.

I told her how we lost each other
On the porch when your daddy saw us kissing,
And the rain began to fall.

I was alone and you were so far away,
Just down the street and around the corner.
We didn't dare pick up the phone when it rang.
We didn't dare change before class or sit in the scary hall.

We didn't dare look at each other in church but still
The other girls laughed.

Everything I said at home was somehow wrong.
They blamed you for my grades.
They called you troubled and said that it was for the best
When your parents stopped taking you to church.
I lost my way.
I lost my heart.
I lost my faith.
I lost my key to the lock.
I lost my only love when they found you in the creek behind the trestle.

Oh, Sherry, it was the '80s,
When kids played games like truth or dare and all the songs were about us,
And each Friday was nights under the covers and lights out and
It was never something to laugh about.
Hold on, hold on.

I told her about the day I had to stay home
When everyone in our church threw flowers at your feet,
And lies were spoken over the Book of Life.

I would be fine, they said, because I was strong,
But you were the brave one.
I was afraid of their eyes and their words,
And afraid of the pain,
But I didn't dare follow you for fear
That what they said was the truth.
I lost too much when I lost your smile,
And never again sat in the scary hall.

Oh, Sherry, it was the '80s,
When you were like a cat in the dark and then you were my darkness,
And all the days and all the nights became one long, lonesome prayer;
Wait for me in Heaven, my first and only best friend.
Hold on, hold on.

— FOLLOWING —

Farther than to know, yet closer than to see;
Solos, and duos, and less the more.
Wanderings, overgrown, walks dappled—
The trees; taller than to live, yet speaking not to takers of the forest.

There is no straight way through the long unkempt garden
Names called lose their way; echoes are for naked stone.
Faces searched for now in shimmering pools
Move their lips, but remain as silent as the giants.
Warmth is more elusive;
Breeze by the night side fire, drops of morning diamonds
Touch the shoulder where once a lock of hair rested.

Footsteps unguided can still be found at the sunlit temples
Rising between the unknowing, the almost seeing;
   Visions of the smoke of spruce,
     Scents of earth and growth.
Tell nothing of who came before
Nor hint of the place where
They left the path.

— INCONSTANT MOON —

for fire does in this life light
your face in its softness
arising through folds of quilted cotton
one side to the fairy flame
the darker side to me.
I ask you to turn and tell me what you see
but the shadow doesn't turn with you
so wanes the light
then crescent
then silhouette
then eclipse
and the annulus whispers
come to me.

— IF I WERE ASKED WHAT I WANT —

I want to bring something uncertain to
doors and stairs and what falls slowly through and down and up them

I want to speak the words that bring sweet tears to
cars and cubicles and cyclone fences and brick facades and all the hungry
       and lonely
emptiness that call them home.

I want to raise a hammer and drive madness into
idle hands and happy feet that build only things and dance only steps
taught under the lights of neon beer signs.

I want to retire comfortably in the knowledge that lovers still cuddle
with cheeks covered in playfully stolen kisses
innocent of dreams shattered and hearts crushed
near a slowly dying campfire
at the hidden lake.

— SWALLOW ME UP —

swallow me up
you river fish
tear my flesh
which only hurts
above my heart
rip
the muscles long since last used
from bones so often bowed so often bent so often
break
up the bits and
share them out
give
to hungry brothers and starving sisters
until the giving hurts
someone else.

— THE MYSTERY —

Be it soft, sudden, strained, or unsought;
There is nothing in human interaction
So frightening
So fulfilling, frustrating, assuring, dangerous, tempting, torturous or
So sublime as
That first kiss.

By lips, yet unvoiced;
Face to face, yet unseen,
It is the replacement of dreams into reality and reality into dreams.

— OTHER PLACES NO ONE SEES BUT FEELS —

Nothing steals as much as
Mornings spent napping
So far on the way to
Being together
So simple and yet
Heart too hard to hold
To do anything
To say all that needs to be
Held in mind and soul and
Other places no one sees but feels
No one hears but still falls.

Never you mind
This is but looking in from too far outside
Burn for him
For her
For fire does in this life light
More than faces
For warmth of skin on skin
Burn for him
So simple and yet

No one hears
But still falls.
Never you mind
There's a reason why love is deaf as well as
Mornings spent napping
Two is better than one
Never say no when
Sunrise catches you together.

To do anything
To feel more and more
To burn
This is what we burn for
When the sunrise catches us alone.

So simple and yet
You must fall
There's no other way to know
So fall.

— SUICIDE HILL —

street smarts and book smarts and
nothing smarts like a skinned knee
and nothing breaks like
going too fast
down the wrong side of the hill
top to bottom in ten seconds
flat on your ass and tumbling
head over heels over head over
please, just give me time to catch
my breath my thoughts my
what big eyes you have
all the better to eat you with
no gears and no brakes and no wings and no rules
and nothing breaks like
little boys on wheels.

— FRAGILE —

Quickening her step, the grad student hurries from under red oak darkness
  to mercury vapor light, but
The whispers don't recede.
Her shadows crawl under her shoes, but
The faces don't dissolve.
She clenches her fists on her purse string, her key ring.
She closes her eyes, hoping that when she opens them . . .

Both Jimmie's and her shoes were already soaked, so they took them off
  and waded through the creek barefoot.
Green on rocks, toes slide over—cool water to her ankles, under the cuffs
  and up her calves.
Jimmie was so serious, looking for the fossil he'd seen the day before.
She didn't care as long as he took her with him.
He spoke—frustrated—the roots covered the part of the bank where he'd
  seen it.
She laughed as her foot slipped off of the higher bed, but there was sand to
  catch it.
Her jeans wet to her knees, the coolness crawling in between them.
A yelp that startled her—Jimmie thrashing, then still—he'd found it.
She waded closer, deeper, to see.
Jimmie—without moving aside—pointed to a large, dull stone jutting from
  the bank
In the shadow of the tree's roots.
The roots under the water brushed her now soaked waist, but
Jimmie's smile was too bright for them to follow the cool water in.
He turned and began tearing at the brown earth now two feet below the
  grass.
She hadn't time to see what the stone was before he got in the way.
She pulled away from the roots, a hand strangely lifting from the water
To wet the back of Jimmie's Ocean Pacific shirt.
Oblivious, he scratched and pulled, his arms stronger than they looked in
  school.
She caressed his warmth, his backbone, his muscles moving under his
  shoulders.
Jimmie fell back with a yelp as different from the first as

His open mouth was from his smile.
The stone, pieces of earth still clinging, hit the water at the same time
Jimmie's body pushed her hand aside and
Slid beneath the wave it made.
For a breathless moment, she saw Jimmie's eyes wide,
Moving in ways only water moved, but
They were too bright.
When she opened her own, below the water, still wavering from the
    disturbed surface,
A large stone sat on the sandy bottom.
Although she could see between the shadows of the roots that he had found
    what must have been the largest snail which had ever lived,
Jimmie was gone.
In all the places within her where his warmth had touched, the cool water
    flowed.

At least one of the faces would be his.

— FALLING BY THE WAYSIDE —

Along this lonely road I know
There rarely have been others,
Much love of life it's drained from me
Much growing sight it smothers.

Many worlds this road has led to,
And many lives I've known;
But, it means nothing, my heart tells me
Unless someone I've shown,

The magic of love at dawn . . .

A garden of stone—the real world gone;
The effect of a young girl's tear.
The warmth of a touch with a stab of fear;
The music only the blind can see,
How beautiful life can truly be.

— LILY —

Once was a young girl
Delighted at prancing and dancing
Over the soft earth and through the warm grass
Of her father's farm.

She found there at five
A tiny gold flower, barely alive
Clinging to the river's side
So she took it up and showed it to her father's tired eyes.

Grew and showed anew
Every year's impossible
Return to the life, now no larger than her fingernail.
Next as wide as her delight
Yet always on just one day in the bright sun.

A woman now stood, beside her father's rest
Stood with a dewy tear to see her lonely friend
Bowing his haloed face toward her sorrow
On this, his one glorious day.

Never did she invite another to join her at the river's side
Never did she look across the flowing water
But only picked the flower each year
The bloom that only she could see.

And, finally rested there beside her father
Beside the clearness of icy tailings
At her head one shivering, golden marker . . .
At last left to go to seed.

The next spring saw two coins where for a lifetime shined only one
There years later, the graves overgrown, the banks teeming with
    shimmering gold.
When a tiny child, brought by her doting daddy, to wash her dirty hand at
    the water.
Its cold splashed playfully on face and father's alike without knowing on
    whose bed they sat.
She reached out to grasp a flower there, the valley-wide harvest of another
    life.

— I AM BECOME MAN —

First the waking
From star sleep,
Then the quaking
Ten thousand fathoms deep;
First the fall
Then swimming free
Brings into thrall
Beached botany
Your seeds to keep.

Second eyesight
Gives open prey;
The arc light shark bite
Takes it away.
Second to nothing
Years gained through thought
Not long become a king
On wings you have bought;
Sail into the day.

Third from the left
Behind and below
Come the bereft;
Two, stupid and slow.
I in my cursive
And you with your trap
We cannot both live
Past cold thunder clap
In Pele's hallow.

Forth boils the milk
Once again a birth
Enfold the child in silk
For all who know his worth.
The end of the matter
In the heat of the Son,
So the world we will shatter
With the primal war won;
Life versus the Earth.

— UNTITLED —

There's a tear in the eye of the man in the moon,
But not for me.
I'm not a threadbare soul
To sigh for,
I watch as he watches
The interminable comings and goings
Of what passes for relationships,
And the flailing attempts
Of the tragically hip,
To influence, however, perverse,
The untried libidos of the young.

I sigh as he sighs
At the negligent slanting
Of yet another young scruff's
Sense of cultural awareness
By the white boys in blue
In streaking white,
Spawning blood-soaked rules
Into the darkest corners
Of the brightest minds.

I wait as he waits
Waxing and waning
For the wash of emotions
Unknowingly and osmotically
Unleashed from
Endless hours of love-touch posing
By assumingly satisfied couples
And couple wannabes.

I wish as he wishes
Upon a sparkling little dog star
Where all the little people
Hold all the little conversations
That seem to run all the time,
But not for me.

There's a tear in the eye
Of the man on the stage

But not for me.
I'm not the last great American poet
Lying down in the gutter
Of a lost, gray western town
On the broken crust
Of our not-so-heavenly body.

I see as he does
The telltale stalls
Of a misbegotten age
On the backside
Of the last great American poet.

I smell as he does
A token of the hopelessness
Blossoming from the hundred-proof mouths,
The vine-ripened eyes,
And the star-stalled points
Of the last great American poet.

I feel as he feels
The love-soaked fear
Of banging, losing, and forever leaving
All but the little dreams
That the little people
Share in the wee-small hours of morning
At the little dog star
Where nearby lies reality
By the unjust form
Of the last great American poet.

I know as he knows
The meaning behind the words
Of the little conversations
Never shared but overheard
Just out of the line of sight
Of the slowly narrowing eyes
Of the last great American poet.

There's a tear in the eye
Of the man in the clouds
But not for me.

— WHITE ROOM —

In the white room with black curtains in the station
Black roof country—no gold pavement—tired things
Silver horses ran down moonbeams in your dark eyes
Light smiles—are you leaving my contentment?
I'll wait in this place where the sun never shines
Wait in this place where the shadows run from themselves.

You said no strings could sever you at the station
Platform ticket—restless eyes—goodbye windows.
I walked into such a sad time at the station
As I walked out felt my own need, just beginning.
I'll wait in the cue when the trains come back
Fly with you where the shadows run from themselves.

At the party she was kindness in the hard crown,
Consolation for the old fool now forgotten.
Yellow tigers crouched in jungles in her dark eyes.
She's just dressing—goodbye windows—tired starting.
I'll sleep in this place with the lonely crowd
Lie in the dark where the shadows—you know!

— PERISHABLE —

Four o'clock and that's all I've got;
Twenty minutes until ten years gone.

Reach out while young,
Or those who got away will lose their faces
As well as the feeling of their hands in yours.
Those things aren't supposed to be
Perishable.
But all things pass . . .
And keep reaching out,
Because holding hands is not just for playmates
Or first time lovers;
Even the most jaded can find warmth
In a touch.

— PSYCHE OPTICKS —

Come dance with me
In the land of demons
The home of the dragons
At the bottom of the sea
In the cliffs.
Come breathe the fire
Of a stolen green morning
In a stone forest
On the shelf.

I await the coming of the comet
With fern at my feet
And feathery serpents swimming in air.
Let me take you there
Into the heart of the heat
Of the dragon's lair.

I live to pull down the giants
My brothers the walking gods of slaughter
The possessors of spinal skin
Help me bring them again
To the womb of the daughter
Of the sun of the sin.

I call to the voice of the mountain air
And answer for my life at last,
The molten darkness cares not.
Give me new weapons of thought
To pay the price for the past
And save the land for which I fought.

Come dance with me
On the grave of the tyrant
The king of the dead
Who planted his headstone
Under the waves.
Come play in the solid surf
And swim the river of fire
In the days of the dragons
The past enslaves.

— GIRL —

Young.
Soft.
Looking
Unnaturally innocent.
Deceptive. Walks with an air
Of defiance. Sees with eyes
So deep. What does she know
That I don't?
I watch her watching me
In someone else.

— A LIVING WILL —

I have no wondrous dreams fulfilled
To offer for your hand,
Nor cold stones to lay upon your breast
Or castles built of sand.
I only have one fine gift
That I may give to you
Which is naught but me myself,
And all my love forever true.

I give you my eyes to close and kiss
And softly I enter a new world blind
And need not see the old one die.
Your lips may brush against my cheek
Now flushed with nervous burn.
Please claim my right and the other
Toward your touch I'll gladly turn.

A taste of salt upon my brow
You arouse my primal sea
It's your blood flowing through my veins
And the seed we soon will set free.

A question beckons from your heart
And passes into mine.
With a smile, I answer, 'yes'
And once again, you see me shine.

My hands and arms, I give to you
For shelter at your will,
A strong and tender hiding place
Only you can fill.

With them comes my life's breath
To warm you in the cold,
And all the time that I can give
For you to have and hold.

I fall upon my bended knee
And present myself to you,
'Cause only with you
Can I be forever free.

— AN EVENING RIDE —

From lispy dreams of a green-eyed girl I rouse
To hunger-pained cries of a thunderstorm
Beating its carnal beauty against my one window!
So I drag my lazy ass out of bed
And, roll out back to the spices, cactus, and spider webs
Hidden in the shadowed corners of our year-old porch
Somewhere beneath my childhood friend
The oak tree.

I decide not to flood the already benched yard
With artificial incandescence, but instead
Ask the lightening to caress my cigarette.
The glow from this cancer-stick reaches in
As the smoke I cannot see but can feel wraps my head.
I recall a burning sky in a downpour.
I recall—

An evening ride in the fever of spring
Meant to be my senior year;
Free at last from sunset curfews,
My bike carries me south to the sea of houses.

Wedgewood, with more cars than trees
Gleaming on their driveways by the light of street lamps
And stars soon to be snuffed out.
I ride
Smoothly and surely to the end of the city
Down Altamesa where the houses are beached;
Not yet making waves beyond James Avenue.
I cross against the light in full view of the militia cops
Drinking coffee at the Stop-N-Go,
Waiting for Death to strike.
I break the barriers of society,
And heft my two wheeler over a flimsy fence.

Both 20x1.75's hit the untried pavement at the same time
On the illegal side—a trespass, I know, but who's to care?
Soon it will be as busy as the rest of the main drag.
Just a slab of progress overstepping its bounds
Then bringing with it the four-wheeled bugs to crunch and gorge
On what's left of the Texas prairie.

And away I go out of the failing sunset into a grassy isle,
Waving darkly away from an oncoming storm.
And there it is just off my right shoulder, churning away.
Though the sun's down those clouds still show their white heads
By roiling and softly booming, sending a silvery blush
Between and about each other and wide across the cattle
I know lumber in their pens somewhere but mostly to the south;
For isn't that why there are cowboys in Texas?
And the thunderhead rises but doesn't billow—
It seethes and blossoms and howls like an atom bomb.
The wind whips my handlebars and I smile;
I'm in the path, strapped to a mustang
And this one's going to last for more than seven seconds.

A moment's pause at the end of the road
In the center of a milkweed oasis with discarded newspapers
Prematurely blowing from grass to concrete to grass—
Running for their lives from the wrath of the rain god.
Silly things; should've stayed trees to ride it out,

Tossing and creaking like ships from the old world
Come to bring salvation to paradise.
Now follows a drop or two to remind me of the chill to come
From the angry blanket rolling over my head.
I no longer see the dizzying heights the cloud reaches for
And instead am forced to turn and withdraw
Back along the lonely road—
Back into the lonely city falling over itself to reach the prairie
As savage gusts push and tear at me
And the beast barks and flashes his teeth.
Under disarmingly bright street lamps
The concrete darkens and dampens;
Mother Nature is wetting her lips
And plastering my hair against my brow,
With ever-increasing bursts of lightening;
Drops of icy sky-water; and of course, the wind
Whistling and screaming the death-throes of innocence.

Terra wall oasis all around me now;
Biting landscaping and slowing well-tended lawns;
Scaring shepherds and lap dogs
Banished to their back yards.
Schizophrenic spider web dances through the heavens
Warning of the danger of playing with fire.
Catch me if you can! I cry, rearing my steel stallion—
What a way to die, riding a wheelie in the center of Main Street;
Laughing at yuppies cowering in their bedrooms;
Racing the wind for all that it's worth;
And drenching myself in the tears of our Mother.
This is no whimpering piss on a dawnless day in January,
It's the cold violence of spring and damn the common sense!
It's the ecstasy of lovers coming together for the first time;
The slamming of their bodies rocking the bed,
And don't you know they're drenched in sweat.
As the streets run in rivers
And the adrenaline rushes through my veins;
The eyes of the city wink once and go out completely—
Beaten into submission by the breath of the Almighty.
Electrical rainbows do their work well;

Splitting the night into knife-edged shards,
Stealing the stage from the black noise of the raindrops
That sting like ice pricks and get in my eyes.
Another bright monster piece sets off a chain of cymbals;
A raucous so loud I can't hear the splashes
Of my proud prancing pony
As I dive through the deepest rivers
In the history of parking lots.
But through all the symphony
Of Banshees and drum beats
And buckets of Mother's milk
Blown from the steppes of Russia
I sense despair and foreboding.
'Cause no matter the fury of this woman scorned
Still the drivers risk the streets
And still the houses stand in neat rows
And still the huddled masses settle and grow
And push back the frontier and civilize the savages
And silence their most natural urges.
All but one.

This that fuels the factories building the cities
And leads me to chase and reap the wild wind;
This that finds us all grumbling and huffing away
Our sexual tension in the backs of photos
And Hollywood Hiltons;
This that follows at the heels of the world
And nips and prods until finally
We break into full gallop so it won't tear out our hearts.
This that's in every Miller and Cummings and Price and Prassio
And of course yours truly; though lately more modestly,
The urge of the living to stave off the End.
The flight of the lemmings to the sea and rabbits from the prairie fire;
The change in the miser at the sight of the sickle-bearers
The sweat and the juice of the virgin no longer,
The pain of lost foreskin and hymen and youth
The breath and the bone of humanity,
The joy and furor of the glimpse of immortality,
This that brings me finally shivering and dripping to my own doorstep,

With energy to spare for one final thunderclap—
A knock that brings a rare, foul-mouthed mother;
As surprised at my survival as afraid of my death.
And a lashing of tongues that I earned with audacity
That, I, a mere child, would challenge the rain.
But, oh, mom, if only you'd go out there
And ride a mile in my saddle,
You'd understand what it means to rebel against the establishment
Of cities and all that goes with them.
Instead, I'm sent to the room with one window
To unclothe and return the foul wet things
To their rightful owner for proper care.
I'm sent to my warm, safe bed
Without any supper
To ponder the error of my ways
And regain my senses
So recently awash in the love of the storm.
To fall slowly into the rapid eye movement
And dream of a green-eyed girl . . .

A last solemn drag from the butt of the cancer-stick
Sees but a token flash in the distance.
The rumbling of kettle drums soften with the close of a door
And the drips give way to the hum of central air.
No harsh words face me now though my mind's as rebellious
As ever it once was before.
But the body's less willing to go meet its maker
And unable regardless to mount the steel horse,
So with a last thought of the forces of nature,
I slowly but surely vault into bed.

www.ingramcontent.com/pod-product-compliance
Lightning Source LLC
Chambersburg PA
CBHW071300040426
42444CB00009B/1806